• •

ABC

Tricycle Press
Berkeley • Toronto

Thank you, Jay

Tricycle Press
a little division of Ten Speed Press
P.O. Box 7123
Berkeley, California 94707
www.tenspeed.com

Book design by Tasha Hall

Library of Congress Cataloging-in-Publication Data

Alda, Arlene, 1933–
[ABC]
Arlene Alda's ABC.
p.   cm.
Originally published: Millbrae, Calif.: Celestial Arts, c1981
Summary: A collection of photographs of things in our environment
that resemble the letters of the alphabet.
ISBN-13: 978-1-883672-01-0 hc / ISBN-13: 978-1-58246-073-4 pbk
ISBN-10: 1-883672-01-5 hc / ISBN-10: 1-58246-073-6 pbk
1. English language—Alphabet—Juvenile literature.
[1. Alphabet] I. Title. II. Title: ABC.
PE1155.A45 1993
[E]—dc20   93-24999
                                             CIP
                                             AC

First published by Celestial Arts, 1981
First Tricycle Press printing, 1993
First paperback printing, 2002

Manufactured in China

2 3 4 5 6 — 09 08 07 06 05

Years ago, when I first started taking pictures, I took hundreds of shots of people, animals, landscapes, seascapes, and objects. Everything was of interest to me, without a sense of artistic discrimination.

As I got better at what I did, and as my eye became more discerning, I began to realize that my enthusiasm was being enhanced by developing a selective and expressive eye with my camera. It was with this spirit of selectivity that I began wandering and taking photos of things in our environment that resembled alphabet letters. It was a visual game for me. Ironically, my game-playing and selectivity led me back to a time when I was much less sophisticated.

As a child, I remember looking up at the sky and noticing the clouds as they changed shape and forms. I played the game of imagining faces in those white and grey puffs. Rocks were another rich source of imagined faces, as were water and sand. How wonderful it was to recapture the excitement of those early "discoveries," by looking around with a fresh vision.

To see—as a child. That's what this book is all about.

Arlene Alda

The world is rich in shapes,
textures, designs, and colors.

This book is a visual poem.
It speaks of the ordinary
in a transformed way.

If you look around you,
you might even see…

THE ALPHABET

A

B

cCCc

D

E

F

G

G G

H

I

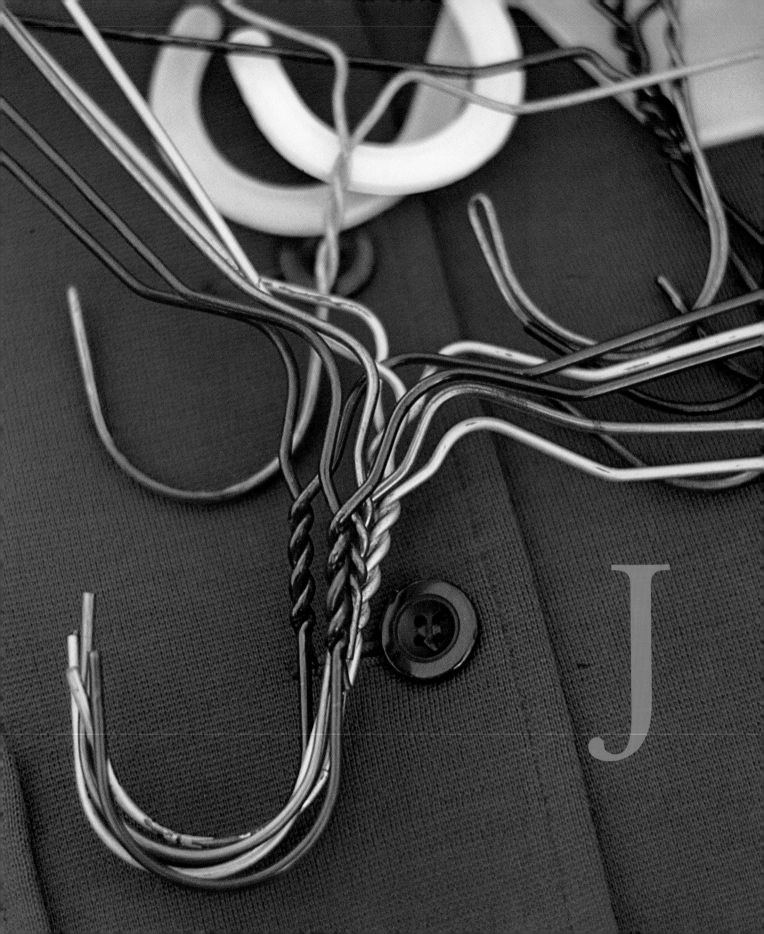

J

K

M

N

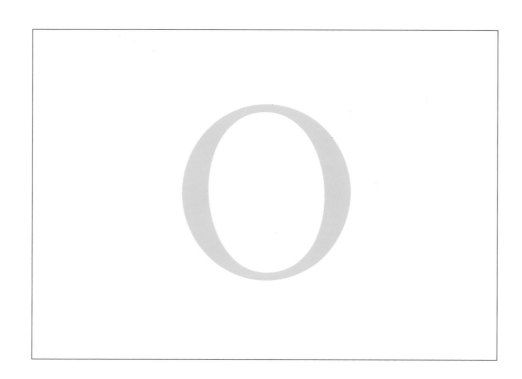

P

R

S

T

$\cdot\ U\ \cdot$

VVVV

X

Y

Z